Path to Pea

Jo Polley

Carbon Writer

Carbon Writer 2018

Path to Peace
by Jo Polley

First Edition: December 2018

ISBN 978-1-9164156-2-1

Publisher
Carbon Writer
carbonwriter.net
publisher@carbonwriter.net
+44 20 3289 1632

Preface

This book is about the need to help.

To help both myself and others.

For myself, it was a way of being heard, something I have felt for many years I needed to do in order to heal. There were things I needed to say to people who either weren't around to hear me or didn't want to hear me, I however still needed to speak. I would often write letters to people with no intention of posting them, yet would somehow get much needed healing and relief in that moment of writing them.

The writing would often be done in poetry form and this too offered the same calm and closure. I kept lots of my poetry locked away in box for many years until a chance conversation brought them to light. The publication of this book enabled me to feel both heard and able to close several chapters of my life that in the past have caused much pain and heartache.

I wanted also to help others. I hoped that in relating to some of what they were reading, adjusting it to fit their own lives where appropriate, that they too could find calm and understanding in confusing situations and some peace for themselves wherever possible. I hope that the reader can see a glimmer of hope on tough days and opportunities to find their own path to peace wherever they can.

I have struggled for many years with both physical and mental pain. Looking back on events, there has always been a thread in my self-help methods - creative output.

In expressing myself in a creative way, in my case it was writing, I have released myself from the grasp of the pain. It doesn't make the pain go away, but it does offer me a different view and will often allow me to distill things down to the real issue.

As you read this, I am sure you will relate to some elements and issues that I touch upon - life is after all, wonderfully complicated.

In publishing my works, which in itself I have found to be incredibly uplifting, it is my hope that I can show you that there is always indeed hope.

Thank you.

Jo Polley,

November 2018.

Acknowledgements

- First and foremost, my *"five family"*. My beautiful children and their dad – my best friends. Thank-you, each of you for being the reason I smile.

- *My Grandparents* – my everything.

- *My dearest Tracey* – thank-you for listening for hours and helping me through to the other end, to the path of peace.

- *NS.* The man who took me as his own and loved me just the same.

- *S* – for supporting me unconditionally and always with a smile.

- *C.S.* The first little boy to make me an auntie. The first child I loved outside of my own children. The little boy who threw me more than any other person ever has, by finding myself in love with someone I'd never met. The little boy I think about all the time.

- *Nigel Derbyshire* – Not just my publisher, but someone who believed in me from the very start, right back to when this book was just a dream. Without you Nigel, none of this would be possible. I will never have enough "thank you's".

- And finally, each and every person who has in some way, however small been the inspiration for my work…whether in a positive or negative way, your input into my life as helped to build me into the person I now am – a person I am happy with and a skin I am happy to live in.

My Work

Jo Polley

The Early Years

Little Dittys

"Little ditty's" is simply a small poem for and about my dear Grandfather. He would burst into song or rhyme at random times and wold have a "little ditty" as he would call them, for all occasions!

I guess I have him to thank for my thirst for poetry!

e always used to sing me songs
and make up funny rhymes.
He'd make me laugh and act the fool,
they were such convivial times!

One more Day

ne more day to love you.
One more day to care.

One more day to stroke your soft skin.
One more day to play with your hair.

One more day to watch you knit.
One more day to hear you speak.

One more day to smell
your perfume.
One more day to see the
rosie in your cheeks.

One more day to wrap
myself in your cardigan.
One more day to rub Oil
of Ulay in your hands.

One more day to play
with your jewellery.
One more day to be my
Nan.

If I could have, just one more thing -
That one more thing would be -

One more day with my precious Nannie,
One more day - Just her and me.

Anxiety

Any time my parents would reminisce about me as a child, on days out to the seaside, and such they would always say "whenever we put you on a ride, you would always be so miserable".

I can still, so clearly remember how (what I now know to be a life time of suffering with anxiety), I would feel in this and other situations. Back then, 30 years ago, I had no idea I was struggling with anxiety and its cruel grip on me. It's only now that I'm articulate enough to express myself in such a way that it was able to be diagnosed. So with that line in mind, I wanted to use it to write about life with anxiety but more importantly, give hope to anyone suffering that in time, with support and being honest with yourself and others, it's possible to find the words to let others around you into your world and try to help and hear you.

here's a little girl on a fairground ride,
She's not laughing, she won't smile.

She's not posing for the camera,
It doesn't seem her style.

She's not doing it to be difficult,
She doesn't want it to be this way.

But this ride is giving her strange feelings,
She hopes that she can explain one day.

She starts to shake and feel nauseous,
It's not because of the ride.

It's because of the strange things happening to her,
Because of the way she feels inside!

That little girl, now a woman,
with children of her own.

She searched hard for the answer
and her confidence has grown!

She now understands the problem,
It's now all very clear.

She now no longer faces situations,
with quite the same dread and fear.

She now knows it was anxiety,
that made her be that way.

It stayed with her, all through her life,
up to this very day.

As long as she can remember,
She's struggled with this "thing"

and all the complications,
that keeping it inside is bound to bring.

She didn't know the words,
or how to get it out.

But, now she knows she's had anxiety,
for her whole life - there's no doubt.

But there's a happy ending to this story,
It's not all sad and glum.

She now has a better grip on the problem,
and happier days have begun!

Anxiety is still a problem to her,
it doesn't go away.

But now she can control it better,
with support along the way!

Jo Polley

Teenage Years

The Silent Scream

 shout louder and louder,
But inside, it's a scream.
A scream to be noticed,
I feel trapped - in a bad dream.

Inside, I am begging,
To be heard, to speak out.
Really, all I want is some calm,
I really don't want to shout.

I'm confused and I'm lonely,
I don't know how to express -
My feelings of upset,
of pain and of stress.

I know what I need to say,
I know what I need to get out,
But, I don't know how to express it,
So, instead - I just SHOUT!

Jo Polley

Dancing

My 13 year old self

ostumes sparkling - colours aray,
Stage lights bright and dramatic,
Nothing can get in my way.

I'm here - they're watching,
all eyes are on my.
Right now I'm feeling,
there's nothing I can't be.

The freedom of performing,
the emotions it brings,
the art of the movement,
feeling so free from within.

The music invites me,
to be my own kind of self,
The feelings of satisfaction -
like an abundance of wealth.

I'm free when I'm dancing
I'm ecstatic - I shine!
The stage here for me,
Tonight it is mine!

Sit with me on the sofa

my 12 year old self

it with me on the sofa - Please don't walk away.
Sit with me on the sofa - there's something I need to say.

Sit with me on the sofa - you never, ever do.
Sit with me on the sofa - I really do need you.

Sit with me on the sofa - don't get up and leave me here.
Sit with me on the sofa - I need to feel you near.

Sit with me on the sofa - maybe we could hug?
Sit with me on the sofa - please don't stand up and shrug.

Why won't you sit with me on the sofa?
Why do you always stand when I sit by your side?

Again, you walked away from the sofa,
- I went to my room and cried.

Crying

 salty sting on crimson red skin,
A headache pounding like a drum.
A weakness inside, feeling like giving up.
Hopelessness and burning eyes
Crying - the bitter expression of pain.

Adult life

Lonely in a crowded room

he room is full, there's a buzz in the air,
I've already been through such a journey, just
to prepare!
I don't mean my clothes, I don't mean my face,
It's a journey of emotions just to be here in this place.

I smile and I chat, I do all the right things -
to hide the anxiety that a gathering brings.
I laugh and I dance, I make everyone smile,
They haven't a clue that I want to run miles.

I'm not really who, they know me to be,
I'm not really the person they all choose to see.
I'm a lonely, sad child in a big adult shell,

I'm trapped in the nightmare of my own living hell.
There's people in waves, flowing like a human sea,
But really I'm lonely, I'm alone. It's just me.

I'm surrounded by people, but still I'm so sad,
I'm sad and tormented by what could have been had.

I'm sad and I'm lonely, but I mustn't appear dull.
I'm sad and I'm lonely, in a room that is full.

CHRONIC PAINS

Crippling sensations, put a hold on life,

Hopeless feelings and helplessness rife.

Restless nights, no sleep at all!

Over and over, I continuously fall.

Needing assistance, not able to cope,

I'm desperate to be pain free - I live in hope!

Concentrating almost impossible, don't know where to turn,

Pain pushing its way through - a consistent, sore burn.

All at once, life changed - it became hard!

It was like being both physically and mentally scared.

Never does the pain pass, it just eases some days,

So now I've adapted to life different ways.

Christmas Tree

Apart from the obvious joy that Christmas brings some people, Christmas for me was always a time I could predict calm and happy memories.

However difficult family relationships have been both in younger or in adult life, when we've been together in each others lives at Christmas, it's always been a happy time regardless of any difficulties of any kind at any other time that year.

I will be forever grateful to my parents for amazing Christmas' filled with such wonderful experiences, worked so, so hard for by them both. They taught me some lovely traditions as a parent during this special time and all the little things I could do to pass on the magic to my own children. For this, I will be eternally grateful and forever thankful.

 winkling lights, like glistening snowflakes,
sit proudly on each branch.
Every shimmering bauble,
Pirouetting as if in a dance!

Stimulating and scintillating,
mesmerising with allure,
each bewitching trinket placed on with care,
of that you can be sure!

A charming star sits high on top,
with its clinquant glitter all a glow,
each cheerful hanging ornament,
showing off its beauty, down below.

The Christmas tree, with all its graceful charm,
offers me such comfort and release,
A tool to remember happier times,
a short spell of inner peace.

Victory!

Victory is based on a normal day out and about in town with my little boy. Over the last few years, we've experienced all sorts of varying meltdowns in public and many different reactions from passers by - again varying perspectives. "Victory!" is to express the simple yet joyous occasions when we managed to get done wha we need to with minimal upset, something I hope parents/carers of additional needs children will both relate to and take comfort from.

oday we beat autism, we kicked it into touch!
It wasn't by a long way, in fact it wasn't much.

But still, we beat autism today - we showed it who is boss,
It usually leaves us crying, desperate, at a loss.

But today was slightly different, we really won the day,
We managed to go shopping, without it in the way!

Armed with everything we need, to get this dreaded job done,
We got through relatively unscathed, it felt just like we won!

A blanket to hide under, a buggy so as not to walk,
Covered up and hiding - he doesn't want to talk!

A squidgy ball of sensory light, to focus on and calm,
Reigns, straps and belts galore, so as not to come to harm.

A plastic stick to chew on and a rag to hold tight and near,
A favourite, fluffy teddy from home, to take away the fear.

A great big bag of what we need, everything but the
kitchen sink,
A stomach full of dread as always - what will people think?

Will we manage to arrive home tonight, with no one tak-
ing the time,
To tap me on the shoulders and tell me what "I'd do if he
were mine"?

Or give that look of disapproval, the one we often get,
People feel the need to do it, even though we never met!

Everyone has so much advice and some of it is kind,
But sometimes, we just want to shop - Please! If you don't
mind.

I appreciate your kindness and that you're trying to help,
But please let me be on my way, I can see he's starting to
melt!

The longer that you keep me talking and I have to be polite,
I can see a meltdown coming, that will end up in a fight!

But today that didn't happen, I have no idea why -
He appeared to be a "normal kid" and he didn't need to try.

I don't know how it happened, why today he didn't struggle,
Why today didn't end in tears, with everything in a muddle.

But I'm not going to question, I'll take it that we won!
Today we beat autism - and we've only just begun!

Goodbye Grandad

 walk through the door. It's quiet. It's calm.
"Come on through" she says - "You'll come
to no harm".
I take a step in, please don't let it be true,
Please don't be in there Grandad - Don't let it be you!
No! Please not my Grandad, I'm not ready to know.
Not ready for Goodbye, not ready to let go.

I'm aware of each bone in my body, every move that I
make,
My ears ringing louder with each step that I take.
I can feel my heart beating, beating hard and fast,
My memory like a racing slideshow of moments now past.
It takes only seconds to reach the side of his bed,
My heart sinking heavier and fog filling my head.
My palms now sweaty, my knees trembling at speed,
My heart so broken, it feels like it could bleed.

A purple, velvet covering - keeping his dignity intact,
In life such a smart man - suit, tie and always a cap.
I close my eyes tightly, I don't want to see,
Why has this amazing man, been stolen from me?
A hand on my shoulder, an arm linked through mine,
Standing still in this moment - not aware of the time.
A rare maternal moment as we share the same pain,
Standing here together, both feeling the same.
My mother and I, standing here in the room together,
Can't believe that he's gone, he's gone now - forever.

I open my eyes and place my hand on his chest,
He looks so peaceful as he lays here to rest.
His pale, waxy face, so clear and so clean,
A big smile as he's sleeping - like a beautiful dream.
His face tells a story of a man, now pain free.
With my Nan now in heaven, he's where he wants to be.
I bend over to kiss him, he still feels the same,
All that is different, is the absence of pain.

Goodbye Grandad - for now anyway,
It's only until, I see you again some day.
Goodbye Grandad - Thank you for your part
In helping to guide me and giving me a start.
Goodbye Grandad - You've been the very best!
I promise to love you forever, as you lay down to rest.

He's my Baby

A story of the first time I was alone in the hospital room with my newborn baby.

As I'm sure most mothers can relate, I studied him and stared at him for as long as I could, in awe of his beauty and perfection.

It was a grab at some peace and calm between visitors and doctors calling in - a time I will never forget.

Saturday February 13th 1999

 olding him tightly,
Puling him in.

The beauty of my baby,
Overwhelms me within.

His eyes sparkle brightly,
His lashes, so long.

His skin softly blushing,
A bond so very strong.

Sitting here together,
It's just us, here in this place.

I sit staring deeply,
deep into his face.

His beauty amazes me,
He's perfect in all ways.

I can't put him down,
In my arms, he gently lays.

It comes as a shock,
to feel a love so strong.

My heart once mine,
Now, with him it belongs.

In only a second,
My life changed right away.

My life suddenly richer,
from this very day.

She is mine and I am hers

She has a spirit so refreshing,
She knows where she wants to be.
She is passionate and determined,
She lives to be free.

She is head strong and stubborn,
She fights for what she feels is right,
She soars in her own way -
like a bird taking flight.

She is funny, yet clever.
She is a joker, yet deep.
Determined to reach the top -
No obstacle too steep.

She is beautiful in both ways -
both inside and out.
She is my precious daughter -
I love her without doubt.

Crumbling Spine - middle of the night

ike a stretched piece of elastic,
Like burning flesh, leaving its mark,
Like razors slashing the skin,
Like being trapped in the dark.

Like being held down tightly,
Like being tied to the bed,
Like a map of painful nerve endings,
Like electric shocks in my head.

Like a deep wave of spasms,
Like a shower of nails,
Like being pelted with big rocks,
Like trying to stretch a body that's frail.

I'm stuck and I'm hurting,
The pain too much to bear,
I need so much to move,
Just don't know if I dare.

Fibromyalgia

hick fog envelopes me,
Fireworks sounding off inside my skull,
A drilling and a squeezing,
An aching that is dull.

Spasms leave no part untouched,
they ripple through like waves,
I'm wiped right off my feet again,
It will be like this for days.

I can't remember the word I need,
Or what it is I'm trying to get out,
My body trembling from head to toe,
and my head so full of doubt.

My joints burning like a fire,
hot spots appearing on the skin,
The pain showing itself in physical form
The burning from within.

My hands so full of pins and needles,
My feet can't stand anymore,
The pain shoots right up my legs
As I put my feet down on the floor.

I can't remember what's just been said,
I can't take your words onboard,
I'm trying my very hardest though,
Please be rest assured!

Each tiny feeling of human touch,
feels like a pelted stone,
I really want to be held and loved,
but I'm better left alone.

My speech rapidly worsening,
My words becoming more unclear
My body's movements out of control
My heart so full of fear.

My bed feeling like a million nails,
All digging in to me in turn,
No chance of getting comfortable,
Until my body stops the burn.

The burn and pain of a relapse,
Yes, it's a flare up once again
So in this bed, sad and lonely
till it passes, I'll remain.

My baby that wasn't to be

2003

here's a special baby -
A baby I never got to see,
My baby that I never held -
the baby that wasn't to be.

The baby I would never feed,
Or dress in all things white,
A baby who just wasn't able
to win that solo fight.

A baby who is loved no less,
than its siblings already here,
A baby who I may not be able to hold,
but still hold in my heart dear.

Sleep tight little baby,
Mummy thinks of you every day,
I promise that I'd have fought for you,
If only there had have only been a way.

Stuck!

Sometimes you are stuck in a situation. The problem, is when someone else is keeping you stuck in that situation.

It feels like being physically shackled, and can be just as difficult to escape from or to change.

'm stuck
Like standing in thick black treacle
With chains shackling me tight.

I'm stuck
Stuck in time and in my own nightmare,
I just don't seem to have any fight.

I'm stuck
Stuck and can't change anything,
things just have to be this way.

I'm stuck
Until I can make myself be heard,
it will be like this every day.

It has not been possible to connect your call

rustration,
disappointment,
anger and panic too.

I need to speak,
I need to be heard,
I need to talk to you.

Claustrophobia!

 ick, tock! The cold silent room only allowing the clock to be heard.

The air inside the room is oppressive and angry.
It closes in and allows its walls to touch me somehow.

Gradually, my heart beat is louder than that clock.
it's beating faster and faster, almost ready to burst through my chest.

My hands sweaty and my ears ringing like church bells on a Sunday morning.
The ringing becoming louder until, it too is drowning out the compulsive tick of the clock.

My legs just not strong enough to hold me, I clutch to any-thing in sight.
No part of me can keep still, I'm trembling yet frozen still at the same time.

I'm hot, but I'm cold. I'm clammy and I'm fraught.
My chest feels like 100 bricks are on top of it and there's a lump my throat.

I close my eyes and hope it soon passes
I'm Claustrophobic.

Jo Polley

The Present

Please ... if you're listening

"Please ... If you're listening" is a poem about a relationship I have - or don't have.

It's a poem about my acceptance of the fact that it didn't work out as society expects it should be, my sadness that it wasn't possible to save it but more importantly, me asking the person to be happy and live their life to the full with no regrets. This for me, would make me feel much better to know that albeit, it's not possible for us to share life, at least we weren't apart and unhappy with it to make the whole situation even worse.

lease ... if you're listening,
Please, take the time to hear.
To hear me tell you something,
I want to make things clear.

This isn't what I wanted,
or the way I would have chose to live,
It's where we've ended up finding ourselves,
When neither would forgive.

You, can't seem to find a way,
and I am just the same.
We just aren't able to forgive and forget,
for that part, we're both to blame.

I don't really care anymore,
about who is wrong and who is right,
I no longer have any room in my life,
for bitterness and fight.

I have been really hurt by you,
You've hurt me more than anyone I know,
But even though it's been that way,
You've been the hardest person to let go.

But I know letting go, is the best for us both,
It's the kindest way all around,
We both need to get on with life,
Without feeling we are bound.

Bound together is expected,
It's how people think it should be,
That's not grounds for a happy life,
So please - listen to my plea ...

Please do just one thing for me,
Please be sure, you'll see it through.
There's a little something I need from you,
Something I need for you to do.

Please continue your way through life,
being sure you're living to the full in every way,
Be sure you've fulfilled all areas,
as you go through the rest of your days.

Take chances, enjoy life, be happy!
At least then I could grasp,
why it is you left me there,
Without you - In your past.

I'm not blaming you for leaving,
My bitterness, all dried out.
I'm happy now, moving forward,
I'm focused on the future without doubt.

I understand this is the only way,
"together" just doesn't work,
We're just not able to meet half way,
to soothe each other's hurt.

You talked about how it felt for you,
It was hard, I'm sure it must have been,
But I had so much pain inside too,
But it doesn't feel like it was seen.

Not seen but more importantly,
I don't feel like I've been heard,
I never had a chance to open,
my speaking out - always deterred.

So, instead I found my own way,
to move forward with the pain,
I've only one thing left to say,
Only one thing still remains.

Please - live your life in happiness,
Please - make the hurt worthwhile,
Don't get yourself in upset anymore,
Make sure you always smile.

At least, that way my letting go,
Wasn't a decision made in vain,
At least it would be worth the upset,
the loneliness - the pain.

A life without me in it,
was hard for me, to comprehend,
but at least I'd understand it,
If, it meant your own life you did mend.

I will live me life the same,
I'll do it, just as I've asked you.
Living separate, happy lives,
Is all that we can do.

My Home Town

he town sign, such a welcoming sight for me,
It stands firm on the side of the road on my
approach.

The Church, stands proudly in the middle of the town,
Shops busy and bustling all around it.

The public gardens on the corner of the street,
With its bulging blooms and array of colour -
Once a happy place during my childhood.

Old shops, no longer in use, still hold so many memories
for me,
Young and old faces, take me back to a time that feels so
long ago.

Whichever direction I take, I'm warmed by feelings of
familiarity
A place I know well - A place I belonged.

Memories flood back, both happy and sad,
But either way - this is my hometown where my heart will
always belong.

Time for Change

"Time for change" was one I wanted to share to offer hope to anyone feeling there is none. I wanted to be able to be someone's light at the end of the tunnel on days when they can only see dark.
I wanted to be able to offer encouragement to those in need of uplifting.

 woke one morning and realised,
that life is there for me to take.
It could be a happy, colourful life,
every decision mine to make.

The only person who controls my future,
is me and me alone.
It was time to take a leap of faith,
Out there - the big unknown!

But suddenly, I was no longer frightened.
I wasn't afraid, I wasn't scared!
In fact, I couldn't wait to get out there,
I was so ready and prepared!

I'd finally found some peace and calm,
and my life suddenly felt so light!
So I took the hands of my loved ones
and leapt towards our future, so exciting and so bright!

Additional Needs

 won't allow it to define him,
He has so much more to give.

Just because he has quirky ways
and his own special way to live.

He sees things slightly differently,
The world is so different through his eyes.

But even so, he lives life to the full,
He lets nothing pass him by!

He never lets it stop him,
or slow him down in any way.

He gives his all to everything,
each and every special day.

Because each and ever day IS special,
It's a blessing to have him here.

He's show me the world is a beautiful place,
helped me to let go of worry and of fear.

I was carrying so much pain and upset
that my baby boy wasn't the same,

I was holding onto so much guilt
and a stomach full of blame.

"Don't worry mummy -
You didn't do this to me"

"It's just the way that I am,
the way I'm meant to me!"

Never is he bitter,
or sad about how it is.

He just carries on being him,
with all the love he has to give!

With nothing ever stopping him,
or allowing it to slow him down,

He's taught me to see everyone as equal
every single child deserves their crown!

Just for fun

Friday night at "fat club"

here's a line of 30 people,
all wondering their fate.
All nibbling nervously on their finger nails -
Have they put on any weight?

Sharon is practically stripping,
She can't afford the extra pounds,
She's adamant deep inside her cardigan,
Is where the weight gain can be found!

Mary is getting ready with her excuses,
She knows she hasn't tried her best!
If she really has to, she's fully prepared,
to strip down to her vest!

Janice had dinner at her son's last night,
She ate extra slices of pie!
She's frantically trying to think of an answer
and that best way to justify!

Karen won't stop talking,
about her latest all inclusive holiday,
Poor old Sheila stands and nods,
trying hard to get a word in edge ways!

Susan is giving out advice again,
The same speech she gives every week!
"Don't eat too many bananas"
and "Have Saturday as a treat!"

Tracey is star of the week again,
She shows her medal with pride!
But really she can't believe it,
Since the middle of last week, she hasn't really tried!

Sally is a bridesmaid soon,
it's only a few days away!
She's left herself no time at all,
to be a stone lighter on the day!

Lisa is flying off on her hols next week,
She wants a "beach bod" the day she flies,
Trouble in, she can't stay off the cake,
and plenty more besides!

It's Friday night at fat club,
Nothing changes much.
It's crazy, chaotic and hysterical,
But man! I love this bunch!

Tea!

here would we be,
in a world without tea?

Whatever it is you're thinking,
a cup of tea is what you'll be drinking!

With family or with friends,
a cuppa' helps to mend!

A broken heart or a broken arm,
A cup of tea holds so much charm!

There's something about that golden nectar,
That helps to make all things much better!

So, if you're sad and feeling blue,
you know what it is, you must do!

Switch on the kettle and fill your cup,
Before too long, you'll be on the up!

Jo Polley

The Flower

ake some time to notice,
the beauty of a bloom.

Each silky, textured petal,
like a light and delicate plume.

each little bud, pushing open
and bursting its way into the light.

Its ever-changing colour and its perfume
to please and to excite!

The way it leans and forms itself,
the way its beauty lights up a room.

Have you ever taken the time,
to appreciate, the beauty of a bloom?

Chocolate

eep, dark, satisfying indulgence,
dancing and tantalising on the lips.
Its sweetness and its richness
like tiny pieces of opulent bliss.

Each mouthful more pleasurable than the last,
a moment to be fully absorbed and adored
this is your moment, just for you,
your luscious, carefree conspicuous reward!

Jo Polley

Mum Life!

uuuum!!!! Mum! Where are you?
My bother's just spilled his drink!

Muuuum!!! Come quick to the kitchen,
the cat's just been sick, I think!

There's biscuits trodden in the carpet
and juice all over the floor!

My sister's stormed upstairs with the huff
and the Postman's at the door!

There's sticky stuff all over the window,
it wasn't there a moment ago,

I thought I better tell you,
I thought you'd like to know!

The dog is howling at the neighbour,
there's something really wrong.

He's digging a big hole under the hedge,
he'll be round there before too long!

There's jigsaw pieces all over the playroom floor,
I don't know how they got here,

The laundry basket has been tipped upside down
and there's socks all up the stairs!

Muuuum !!! I've lost my homework book,
I think it's in outer space!

Unless, you've done what you always do,
and put it somewhere, in a safe place!

Muuum!!! What's for tea tonight?
I feel like I'm wasting away!

Muuum!!! Come and cook my tea please,
I want to get out to play!

Muuuummmm!!! Come quick,
I don't know what to do!

Alright! OK! I'm coming!
I'm only on the loo!!

Jo Polley

The Future

The dream that came true

Because you believed in me

had a dream some years ago,
but no confidence to see it through.

It's because you believed in me,
that my dream is coming true.

I don't know how to thank you,
words don't seem enough to convey -

The gratitude I have for what you've done,
for helping me on my way.

The Future

here do I see my future?
Of that I have no idea.

But I do know as long a I have family,
I have nothing I need to fear.

Thank you

A dedication to my Husband

hank you for always being there
and staying right by my side.

For sitting close beside me,
on this often bumpy ride.

For picking up the pieces,
of my often broken heart.

For being my every source of comfort,
for covering all parts.

All parts of what I need and crave
for being all people rolled into one.

For being my source of support and love,
since this path to peace of mine begun.

Jo Polley

Jo is a wonderfully warm person, with a complicated and textured past, who has found inner peace.

With the support of her 3 children, loving husband and sheer determination, she has rekindled her written voice, and created a new passion to share her poetry.

Jo wants to show others that no matter what life serves up to you, it is possible to find islands of calm which may indeed lead to their own path to peace.